D0182649

Usborne Naturetrail

Please return / renew by date shown.
You can renew it at:
norlink.norfolk.gov.uk
or by telephone: 0344 800 8006
Please have your library card & PIN ready

NORFOLK LIBRARY
AND INFORMATION SERVICE

NORFOLK ITEM

30129 065 262 017

A female emperor
dragonfly laying eggs

Usborne Naturetrail
Insects
& other creepy-crawlies

Rachel Firth and Louie Stowell

Designed by
Michael Hill and Marc Maynard

Illustrated by
Dan Pearson, Non Figg
and Ian Jackson

Edited by Jane Chisholm and Susanna Davidson

Consultant: Dr George C. McGavin,
Oxford University Museum of Natural History

Usborne Quicklinks

The Usborne Quicklinks Website is packed with thousands of links to all the best websites on the internet. The websites include information, video clips, sounds, games and animations that support and enhance the information in Usborne Internet-linked books.

To visit the recommended websites for Naturetrail Insectwatching, go to the Usborne Quicklinks Website at **www.usborne-quicklinks.com** and enter the keywords: **naturetrail insectwatching**

When using the internet please follow the internet safety guidelines displayed on the Usborne Quicklinks Website.

The recommended websites in Usborne Quicklinks are regularly reviewed and updated, but Usborne Publishing Ltd. is not responsible for the content or availability of any website other than its own. We recommend that children are supervised while using the internet.

A young
bush cricket

CONTENTS

A high brown fritillary
butterfly perching on
a thistle flower

How to be an insect spotter

Not all the tiny scurrying, creeping or flying creatures you'll see are insects. You can tell an adult insect by the fact that it has six legs and three main body parts, plus a few other bits, such as feelers.

Don't worry about getting confused, though. This section will help you tell the difference between insects and other creepy-crawlies, and between adult insects and their young.

Look up, look down

As an insect spotter, you're spoiled for choice. There's a whole miniature world beneath your feet... and in the trees, and in the air above your head. It would be a tough challenge to walk in the park in summer and *not* spot any insects.

IMPORTANT INSECT SPOTTING TIPS

- Search carefully and try not to harm flowers and twigs when you're looking for insects.

- Always put logs and stones back where you found them. They're often homes for bugs.

- You have a better chance of finding insects if you move slowly and quietly.

- Be patient. You can discover a lot just by waiting and watching.

Large white butterflies like these ones are very common, especially in gardens, woods and fields.

A creepy-crawly world

We tend to think of Earth as our own planet, but humans are vastly outnumbered by insects. For every single human being, there are 1.5 billion insects. And that's before you start counting other kinds of creepy-crawlies, such as spiders, snails and worms. (There's more about those on pages 12-13.)

There are about a million known types of insects in the world and thousands of new species of insect are discovered every year. Scientists estimate there might be up to eight million different types of insects, so the ones we already know are just the tip of the iceberg.

Man's pest friends

Insects can be our worst enemies and our best friends. They munch on crops and spread diseases, but they can be very helpful, too. They're nature's recycling team, getting rid of waste so it doesn't pile up.

Dung beetles eat animal dung. So do their young.

Earthworms help break down rotting leaves into soil.

Burying beetles bury the bodies of small animals such as frogs.

AMAZING FACTS

- If a beetle fell off the Empire State Building it wouldn't die, it would bounce.

- Some ants "milk" insects called aphids, stroking them so they release a sweet liquid called honeydew. This sounds pretty, but it's aphid poo!

- Hungry bugs eat 20 per cent of all the crops humans grow. That's two out of every ten fields.

They may not look as cute as other creatures, but insects are very creative. They build nests, make paper, cause explosions, cultivate gardens, capture other creatures as slaves, and even farm them, just like we farm cattle.

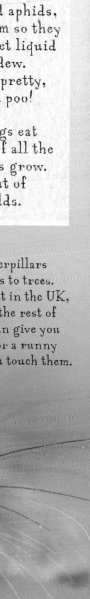

Gypsy moth caterpillars are serious pests to trees. They are extinct in the UK, but common in the rest of Europe. They can give you watery eyes or a runny nose if you touch them.

Introducing insects

INSECT FACT

Most insects have wings, which allow them to zoom up, up and away from creatures that want to eat them. This doesn't always help if a bird is after them. In that case, staying still is usually safer.

You'll see some insects more often than others, so it's good to learn to spot these first, then move on to bugs that are trickier to identify.

Here are some common insects that you can easily spot in gardens, in parks, in the street – or even inside your house.

Brown hawker dragonfly

Red admiral butterfly

Seven-spot ladybird

Rose aphid

Black garden ant

What is an insect?

It's easy to tell if the animal you're looking at is an insect - just count its legs.

All adult insects have six legs and their bodies are divided into three main parts. Each insect also has a hard shell around its body, called an "exoskeleton". You can't always see this, though, as it's sometimes covered with fluffy hairs.

INSECT BITS

The three parts of an insect's body are the head, the thorax (the middle bit) and the abdomen (the end bit). They also have feelers called antennae.

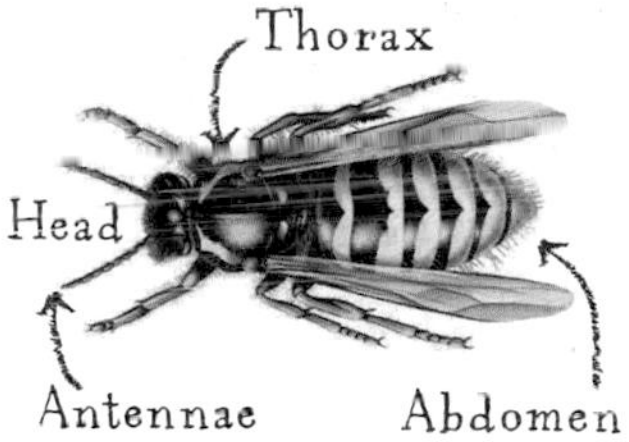

Thorax

Head

Antennae

Abdomen

Common blue butterfly

Peacock butterfly

Shield bug

Stag beetle in flight

Bumble bee

SPOTTER TIP

Look under stones in woods, gardens and fields. If the stone hasn't been moved for a while, a lot of creatures will have taken shelter under it. You'll uncover a writhing, scurrying minibeast village.

Looking for insects

It's not hard to find insects. Often, they find you first. At a picnic, you nearly always get uninvited guests of the creepy-crawly kind. If you leave dirty dishes lying around, it won't be long before flies come buzzing.

Insects are almost everywhere: in gardens, in the street, in fields, in ponds, in sheds and underground. Being so small, every nook is a potential bedroom for an insect.

Each type of insect naturally lives in a place that has the food and shelter that suit it best. This is known as its habitat. Gardens and parks are habitats for all kinds of creatures.

You might find ants looking for sweet, sticky things in your house.

Look for pond skaters on ponds.

Watch for ladybirds attacking aphids among the roses.

Slugs are often in vegetable patches.

Look out for butterflies laying eggs in nettles.

Beetles like to shelter in woodpiles.

When to look

Spring and summer are the best times for insect spotting. That's when the air buzzes with wasps, bees, flies and shining dragonflies, and the grass is alive with beetles and ladybirds

The insect world is quieter in late autumn and winter, but there are still a few bugs out. Winter moths and November moths can be seen sitting on tree trunks after dark – so take your torch and have a look in the garden. On very mild winter days, you might see bumble bees.

This November moth can be seen from September to November.

Many insects spend the cold months asleep somewhere safe, such as inside a log or underground. This long doze is known as hibernation. A good place to look for hibernating creatures is in grass tussocks – raised tufts of grass in fields.

Other insects die at the end of the summer, after laying their eggs in a sheltered spot. The eggs then hatch out in the spring.

Spring

Insects emerge as it grows warmer, hatching out of eggs or waking up after their winter sleep.

Summer

You will see hundreds of insects of every shape and size in the summer months.

Autumn

It's still a busy time for insects. Slugs, snails and worms love damp weather.

Winter

Very few insects appear in the coldest months, but you may see some flies and moths.

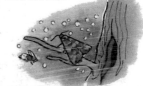

Using a field guide

Field guides are often laid out a little like this, with a picture of each bug and some information about it.

Before you start using your field guide, it's a good idea to see how it's laid out. Most guides have a section for each group or order of animal. For each species, the guide will usually give the "common" name in English (if it has one), and the international scientific name, which is in Latin.

MEADOW BROWN BUTTERFLY
Maniola jurtina

The Latin name is shown underneath.

HABITAT Grassland
FOOD Various grasses

FLIGHT
May-September

WINGSPAN
50-55mm

Entries for butterflies and moths usually show the caterpillar too.

Bug sizes are written in millimetres. Butterflies are measured by their wingspan

HANDY HINT

Good guides will tell you how to tell the difference between similar-looking species. This is useful when you're um-ing and ah-ing about what kind of creature you're looking at.

The entry for each creature should have a description to go with the picture, pointing out things like its shape. Your guide should also tell you how big it usually is, where and when you might expect find it, how common it is, as well as some basic facts about its habits and life cycle.

Different shapes

When you're identifying an insect, look at the shape of its body and wings (if it has them). This will help you work out where to look for it in your field guide. If it has wings, it is almost certainly an insect. If it has just one pair, it will probably be from the order of insects called true flies or Diptera (the Latin name). Some guides list the orders in Latin.

You might want to do some rough sketches of insects when you're out and about, and look them up later. Start off with the basic body shape, like this:

1. Draw an outline of the head, abdomen and thorax.

2. Then, if the insect is still there, add details such as antennae or jaws.

3. Add more details, such as wings.

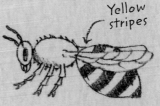

Yellow stripes

4. When sketching, it's a good idea to note down what colour an insect is, because you probably won't have time to colour in your sketches on the spot.

SHAPE TIPS

True flies (order: Diptera) have two wings. Most insects have four.	 Bee fly House fly
Most beetles (order: Coleoptera) have hard wing cases. Look for the tell-tale line down the middle, where the wings fold together.	 Click beetle Great diving beetle
Spiders and other non-insect creepy-crawlies are wingless. Some adult insects, such as silverfish, don't have wings either.	 Cardinal spider Silverfish
If an insect has a "waist" to its abdomen, it's likely to be a bee, wasp or ant. Those belong to the order Hymenoptera - sorry, there's no English name!	 Red ant Common wasp

DETECTIVE KIT

- A notebook and pencil to scribble down your observations and make sketches.

- A field guide

- A digital camera, if you have one, so you can take snaps to study when you get home.

- Insect-collecting gadgets. The "pooter" is a very useful one. You can find out how to make one on the page opposite.

- A magnifying glass. Although you can identify a lot of insects with the naked eye, you'll sometimes need to take a closer look.

Being an insect detective

When you're looking at insects, try asking yourself a few simple questions. The answers will help you identify the creature later on if you don't have a field guide handy.

KEY QUESTIONS...

...to help you identify mystery creatures such as the one on the right, below. Ask:

- How many legs does it have?
Six

- How many sections is its body divided into?
Three. So... it's an insect!

- How big is it?
About a centimetre long.

- What colour is it?
Reddish brown

- Can it fly?
It hasn't yet, but maybe its wings are folded up?

- Any other unusual features?
It's got pincers at the back. Adding together all the evidence, I think it's an earwig.

Common earwig

Earthworm

Making a pooter

A pooter is a tool that scientists use to trap insects without hurting them. It works like a mini vacuum cleaner – except that you do the sucking – and it's very easy to make your own. Here's how:

1. Cut a plastic tube into a long bit and a short bit. Fix thin fabric over one end of the short bit with elastic, to stop you from swallowing anything.

2. Tape card with holes in it over a small see-through pot. Fix the tubes in the holes using modelling clay.

Make sure there are no gaps.

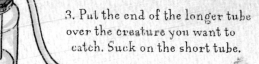

Suck through this end.

3. Put the end of the longer tube over the creature you want to catch. Suck on the short tube.

TRAP TIP

Another way of catching insects without hurting them is to sink a plastic cup into the ground. Insects and other creepy-crawlies that run along the ground will fall in. Don't forget to take the cup out and fill in the hole when you've finished.

1. Dig a hole and put a plastic cup in it.

2. Study the bugs you catch. Then set them free and fill in the hole.

Grasshopper

Meadow brown butterfly

Common wasp

Common snail

Tricky spotter tips

Some creatures are tricky to identify because they look similar to others. A good field guide should help you by pointing out the differences between species that look alike.

Beetles or true bugs?

When you're trying to identify an insect, it helps if you can pick out a feature that shows it belongs to a particular order. For example, if you're not sure if an insect is a beetle (order Coleoptera) or a true bug (order Hemiptera), you can look at its mouth.

Beetles have chewing jaws that move from side to side, like pincers, to snip off bits of food. True bugs have pointed, straw-like mouths. Try looking through a magnifying glass if you're not sure.

WOBBLY FLIERS

Some mosquitos and crane flies look very similar, but crane flies are poor fliers. Look out for them wobbling all over the place when they're in the air.

You can see this rove beetle's pincer-like mouthparts here at the front of its head.

This beetle has pincer-like jaws. Beetles also have a pair of hard wings that cover their flying wings.

This true bug has a pointed beak-like mouth. It pierces and sucks the insides out of other minibeasts.

Butterfly or moth?

Butterflies and moths can look very alike. Not all butterflies are as brightly coloured as people think – some are rather drab, while others are only colourful from some angles. Moths, on the other hand, can be surprisingly shiny. The elephant hawk moth is often mistaken for a butterfly because it's pink.

Here are some things to look out for when you're trying to tell them apart.

MILLIPEDE OR WOODLOUSE?

The pill millipede looks very like the pill woodlouse, and they both roll up when threatened.

Look at their tails to tell them apart. The millipede's tail just has one section, but the woodlouse's has a few sections.

Pill millipede   Pill woodlouse

All butterflies fly during the day and not at night.

Butterflies tend to have slender, smooth bodies.

This is an adonis blue butterfly.

Butterfly antennae usually have little lumpy knobs on the ends.

The back of this butterfly's wings are bright blue.

HANDY HINT

To tell if something's a moth or a butterfly, try watching it at rest. Butterflies hold their wings together above their backs. Moths tend to rest with their wings folded flat.

Moths are often rounder and fuzzier than butterflies.

Moth antennae are often feathery and get thinner at the ends.

Moths usually fly at night though some are active during the day too.

This is an elephant hawk moth.

A seven-spot ladybird
about to take a drink
from a droplet of rain.

Watching insects

When you're looking at an insect scurrying about
in the undergrowth, or on a leaf, or in your bath,
you might wonder how insects see the world.
Can they talk to each other? What do they do
all day? This section takes you deeper into the
creepy-crawly kingdom, exploring how insects eat,
smell, fight, breed and move around. As you watch
insects, think about what they're doing. Are they
looking for food, shelter... or maybe a mate?

ON YOUR MARKS

Try setting up your own insect race by carefully placing a few crawling creatures at the centre of a circle of paper. Do all of them move? Which one reaches the edge of the circle first?

You could put obstacles in their way, such as twigs and stones. How do different insects react?

WALKING ON THE CEILING

Flies can walk on the ceiling because they have sharp claws on their feet which hook into tiny crevices. To help them stick firmly, even on very smooth surfaces, they also have sticky pads on their feet.

Moving around

When you are trying to spot insects, they will be whizzing around a lot of the time. Insects are maestros of movement. Walking, jumping, flying, swimming – you name it, they can do it, and often more spectacularly than any other animal. Watch how different creatures move, so you can identify them more easily.

Grasshoppers have springs in their knees which enable them to jump high.

Jumping high

If you disturb a grasshopper, it will jump high into the air to escape you. Grasshoppers and crickets have long legs and can leap several times their body length. But that's nothing compared to fleas – they can catapult themselves 100 times their own height.

Pushmepullyou

Caterpillars move with a rippling action. They expand (stretch out) and contract (squeeze in) their muscles to move along. They may look as if they have loads of legs but, actually, they only have six. They're all bunched up near the caterpillar's head. All the rest are false legs, called prolegs, which have bristles on them to help the caterpillar grip surfaces as it trundles along. If a caterpillar is in a hurry, it may abseil down on a silky thread which comes out of the saliva-making parts in its mouth.

You can clearly see this hawk moth caterpillar's true legs near its head.

How they move:

Millipede
Millipedes move slowly, appearing to glide across the ground. Each of their pairs of legs take it in turn to step forwards in a wave-like movement.

Ant
Ants move three legs at a time. They move the front and back legs on one side and middle leg on the other side. Then they do the same on the other side.

Worm
A worm moves by stretching out the front half of its body and pushing through the soil. It then pulls its back half up towards its front half.

Flea
Fleas have rubbery pads connected to their legs. They're squeezed tight when the flea's still. To jump, the pads are released, and the flea hurtles forward.

Snail
Like a caterpillar, a snail moves with a rippling motion. It has a big muscly foot which expands and contracts to make the slug move.

Looper moth caterpillars are the only caterpillars not to move with a rippling action.

Front legs   Back prolegs

The caterpillar brings forward its back prolegs, to meet its front legs.

It moves forward by then stretching its front legs away from its back legs.

Wonderful wings

Insects were the first animals to fly, and wings have been the key to their success story. Flying means insects can cover more territory when looking for food or mates, and it also helps them search for new homes or escape from enemies.

Hover flies beat their one set of wings rapidly to hover over flowers while they feed.

Types of wings

Most flying insects have two pairs of wings – forewings in front and hindwings behind. But different insects move their wings in different ways. This means you can learn to identify insects by the way they fly.

INSECT DAREDEVILS

Next time you are near a lake or a stream, look out for shimmering dragonflies. They are the fastest flyers in the insect world and can speed along at up to 50kph (30mph). They can also hover like helicopters and loop the loop.

Most insects have their two sets joined together. They move at the same time in the same direction.

Damselflies have two sets of wings which can move independently of one another.

Beetles only use their hindwings for flying. Their forewings are hard, and act as protective cases for the hindwings when they're not flying.

Unlike all other insects, true flies have just one pair of wings, which move up and down at the same time.

Underwater swimmers

Many insects can swim underwater, and some can breathe in water too. For example, damselfly nymphs breathe through feathery gills, just as fish do. Others take their own air supply down with them, by trapping bubbles of air under their wings or bodies.

Diving beetles scuba dive right down to the bottom of ponds and lakes to catch prey, such as small fish and frogs. They take a bubble of air with them, and come back up when it's used up.

Water spiders also take an air bubble when they are underwater. You can see them swimming upside down, just below the surface.

You'll find insects on the surface too. Look out for pond skaters and whirligig beetles.

FANTASTIC FACT

Water scorpions have an in-built snorkelling tube to breathe through. It sticks out of the hind end of their bodies.

Whirligig beetles swim on the surface looking for food.

Pond skaters are so light, they can walk on water.

Water boatmen move their back and middle legs like oars.

Dragonfly nymphs breathe through gills in their bottoms.

Great diving beetles have hairs on their legs that act like flippers to help them swim.

SNACK FACT

Flying creatures need more energy than crawling ones. This means that nectar, the sweet juice that flowers produce, is a popular meal for all kinds of flying insects.

Insect munchers

For insects, the world is one big feast. They'll happily munch through all kinds of things that don't sound like food to us – wood, blood, decaying flesh and even dung.

Insects and other creepy-crawlies go where the food is – so the easiest way to spot a particular type is to find out what they like to eat.

Who eats what?

SPIDERS

Spiders are meat-eaters. Most eat other creepy-crawlies and many trap prey in webs.

Spider feasting on trapped prey

BUTTERFLIES

Butterflies don't eat solid food. Most drink sweet nectar from flowers.

Small tortoiseshell butterfly

Ice plant

SLUGS AND SNAILS

Slugs and snails eat leafy plants. This means they're often seen as pests by gardeners.

Garden slug eating a leaf

ANTS

Ants love sugary things like fruit, but they mostly eat other creepy-crawlies.

Ants carrying off a dead insect

BEES

Bees drink nectar and eat pollen, a powder found in flowers.

Honey bee feasting on pollen

BEETLES

Most beetles eat leafy plants, but some eat seeds, fruit, wood... or other small animals.

Violet ground beetle

How to catch prey

Meat-eating insects use cunning tactics to catch their food. The zebra spider creeps up slowly on its prey, then pounces like a cat. With surprise on its side, it can even overpower insects that are twice its length, such as mosquitos. Other spiders take a less direct approach and build complex, beautiful webs to trap their dinner.

Web-watch

Look closely at the shape of a spider's web, spread across a hedge or in the corner of a dusty room. This will give you clues about what kind of spider lives there. You can search for that kind of web in your field guide, even if you can't see the spider itself. Here are a couple of common spiders' webs.

This garden spider has caught a wasp in its web and is ready to tuck in.

This is a sheet web made by a house spider. Look for these in sheds or in the corners of dusty rooms.

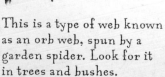

This is a type of web known as an orb web, spun by a garden spider. Look for it in trees and bushes.

BLOOD-SUCKING FEMALES

Mosquitos famously like to feed on people, as well as on other mammals. But it's only the females that do this. The males feed on nectar or honeydew instead.

Insect eyes

If you look closely at a fly's head, you'll notice that it has big, bulgy eyes. These are called compound eyes, and they're made up of lots of little parts – like lots of tiny eyes stuck together. Most insects have compound eyes, but they also have smaller eyes, known as "simple eyes", which you can usually only see with a magnifying glass.

Having lots of eyes doesn't necessarily mean the creature has good eyesight. For example, most spiders have poor vision, even though they have eight eyes.

When you spot an insect, peer at its head through a magnifying glass. What kind of eyes does it have? How many? How big are they?

EYE FACTS

If you move towards a house fly, it'll dart away – its eyes pick up the slightest movement.

Eye stalks

Slugs and snails have eyes on delicate stalks, which they can pull back into their heads.

If you look at a jumping spider closely it will often turn its head and look back at you.

Moths like this privet hawk moth are attracted to lights.

Most of this dragonfly's head is covered by its bulgy compound eyes.

Seeing invisible things

Insects can see a type of light called ultraviolet light which is invisible to humans. Lots of flowers have ultraviolet markings on them, which helps insects to home in on the pollen and nectar.

Watch a bee as it flies up to a flower. It should make straight for the centre. That's because it's following these "nectar guides" to its food. Some other insects, such as butterflies, can see these too.

This flower looks white to us, but the bee sees a landing strip leading to the nectar and pollen-rich middle.

How insects see flowers

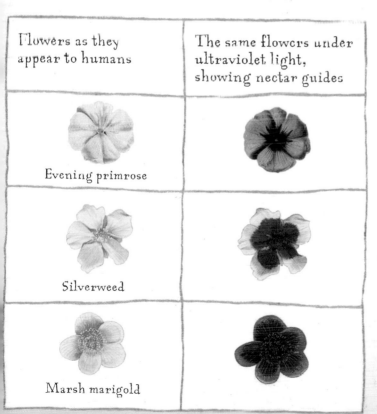

Flowers as they appear to humans	The same flowers under ultraviolet light, showing nectar guides
Evening primrose	
Silverweed	
Marsh marigold	

WASP TIP

If you want to escape a wasp that's coming towards you, try not to move too much. A wasp's compound eyes make them sensitive to fast movements. They'll read your flapping as a threat and might attack.

BUG MOUTHS

Insects' mouths, or "mouthparts", come in different shapes and work in different ways. Here are a few:

House fly

Sucking pad

House flies can only eat liquids. But their saliva can dissolve solid food.

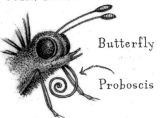

Butterfly

Proboscis

A butterfly's tube-shaped mouth is called a proboscis. It uses it for drinking liquids.

Bee

Proboscis

Bees use a proboscis to suck up nectar.

Taste tests

Insects learn about the world around them in some surprising ways. Although many have at least some of the same senses we do – sight, taste, touch, smell and hearing – they don't always have their sense organs where you'd expect them to be.

For example, crickets have ears in their knees, and flies and other insects taste through their feet. Watch a fly landing on a plate of food. It will often take a stroll around the plate, "tasting" the food with its feet before it settles down to eat.

Proboscis

A butterfly's proboscis works like a straw, slurping up nectar from inside flowers.

Feeling and smelling

Lots of insects have feelers, or antennae, on their heads. These are used for all kinds of tasks, from touching and smelling (insects don't have noses) to sensing how hot it is and whether anything's moving nearby.

When a creature walks or flies, it makes the air move, and insects can pick up these tiny changes in the air around them. Antennae come in lots of different shapes.

MOTH FACT

Male moths have large feathery antennae. Those sensitive feelers can pick up the scent of a female moth miles away.

Antenna

Longhorn beetles have long antennae. They use these to tap trees to find the right spot to lay their eggs.

Bad vibes

Lots of insects have little hairs on their bodies that can sense movement and sound. The stiff hairs on a caterpillar pick up sound waves in the air. Try clapping or whistling near a caterpillar. Watch how it curls up or suddenly "freezes".

As well as picking up vibrations, the hairs on insects' bodies are also sensitive to touch. When one of these hairs touches something, the bug feels it.

Ants send signals to each other by stroking each other. Watch two ants walking towards one another and look out for them getting touchy-feely with their feelers and forelegs.

35

This female glow worm has lit herself up to attract a mate.

Breeding time

It's not surprising that insects outnumber humans by 1.5 billion to one. They can breed at a head-spinning rate: a house fly can produce up to 500 babies in just four days. But it's not all plain sailing. First each insect must find a partner.

Bugs use all sorts of noises, smells and signals to attract mates. Groups of male mining bees even get together to put on a display to attract females. Look out for clusters of them zooming round dead flowers. They flutter their shimmering wings as they go.

TOKENS OF AFFECTION

Male scorpionflies try to attract females by offering them dead insects (often stolen from a spider's web) to prove that they will make good mates.

Laying eggs

If you leave food out in the summer, after a while you may spot tiny white flecks in it. These are fly eggs. Most insects' young come from eggs laid by the female. Different insects lay their eggs in different places.

Scrape away some soil to look for slug eggs just below the surface in moist soil.

Wasp spiders spin a silken bag, called an egg sac. Look for them on vegetation near webs.

Mother love

Once the eggs have hatched, larvae usually have to fend for themselves. But some creepy-crawly babies get more of a helping-hand than others.

Female wolf spiders carry their spiderlings (young spiders) on their backs for up to a week. Earwig mothers lick their eggs to keep them clean. Then, when their young hatch out, they feed them by vomiting up food. But if they haven't left their mother after a week, she will try to eat them!

And it's not just the mothers who help out. Male giant water bugs carry the females' eggs around on their backs. They even keep the eggs clean, by stroking them from time to time.

LONE PARENTS

Unlike most other insects, aphids give birth to live young, rather than laying eggs. Some aphid babies don't have a father. Females can make babies all on their own.

There are dozens of newly hatched spiderlings, huddled together, on this mother wolf spider's back.

From egg to butterfly

A lot of insects change dramatically as they grow. Wriggly young caterpillars become airborne adult butterflies and squishy beetle larvae turn into tough-shelled adult beetles. This process is called metamorphosis.

Look out for insects at every stage in their life cycle. You might see a cluster of eggs on a leaf, or a crawling larva such as a caterpillar. The next stage after that is when the larva turns into a pupa. This is a case that protects the creature as it changes into an adult. Look out for these hanging from plants.

EGG HUNT

If you see lots of a type of butterfly near a plant, see if you can spot any eggs on the leaves. Look on the undersides of the leaves as well as on top.

Holly blue

Here's how the painted lady – a common butterfly – grows and changes.

1. The painted lady butterfly lays its eggs on leaves, often nettles or thistles.

2. The caterpillar hatches, eating until it's fully grown. Then it sticks itself to a leaf with silk.

3. The caterpillar's body splits open, revealing a pupa called a chrysalis.

4. After seven to ten days, this splits and the butterfly struggles out.

FOOD TIP

Adult insects often eat different food from their young. Caterpillars tend to eat leaves, while butterflies sip nectar from flowers. Some adult insects don't eat at all. A good field guide will tell you what a minibeast eats at each stage in its life-cycle.

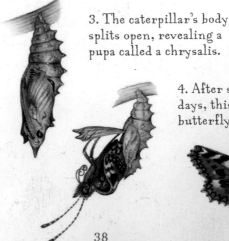

Growing up

Most insects go through the same stages as butterflies do. Although some of them, such as stag beetles, don't come out in the open until they're fully grown. Some creepy-crawlies, especially ones that aren't insects, don't change so much (see page 16).

SECRET CHANGES

A honey bee larva turns into a pupa then becomes a bee while it's still hidden away in the hive, so you'll only ever see adult bees outside. The young adult bee leaves the hive about 20 days after the egg is laid.

1. Stag beetles lay eggs in rotting wood. The larvae hatch and spend three years nibbling on the insides of tree stumps and dead trees.

2. Then the larvae burrow underground and turn into pupae. You might come across stag beetle larvae when you're digging.

3. After about 3-6 weeks, adult stag beetles break out of their pupae, but stay underground for months before they burrow upwards.

When they're fully grown, male stag beetles like these are usually a little under 30mm long.

You can hear grasshoppers singing in fields.

Insect chatter

If you've ever been camping, you've probably heard insects chirping noisily away. But it's not just noise, it's conversation. Male grasshoppers and crickets rub parts of their bodies together to create "songs" that warn other males to stay away, as well as attracting females.

There are quite a few bugs you can "spot" without actually seeing them. In an old house with wooden beams, you might hear a tapping when the place is quiet at night. That's the sound of a death watch beetle. These wood-munching creatures attract mates by bashing their heads against the walls of the tunnels they burrow through old wood.

Male grasshoppers rub their hind legs against their forewings to make a noise to attract a female.

There's an old myth, that the tapping made by the deathwatch beetle means that someone is going to die.

NOISE FACT

The loudest insects in the world are cicadas. Some species sound like a cross between a saw and a knife grinder. They're rare in northern Europe, but more common further south.

Buzz off!

When a bee is attacked or injured it gives off a special scent. This sounds the alarm for the other bees, who buzz about angrily and get ready to sting anything that looks as if it might attack. If you see bees behaving in an agitated way, they might have just got a smelly warning from another bee and you should steer clear.

MATING DANCE

Jumping spiders perform a "dance" before trying to mate. The male waves his front legs around and moves his abdomen up and down, to try to impress the female.

Smell-o-grams

Lots of other insects "talk" using smells. Ants leave trails of chemicals called pheromones for each other, leading to places where there's lots of food. When you see a line of ants marching along, they are probably sniffing their way along one of these trails.

DANCING BEES

If you see a honey bee flying away from a flower, it may be on its way to tell the other bees about the nectar it's found. Honey bees let each other know about food nearby by doing a round dance, like this, inside the hive.

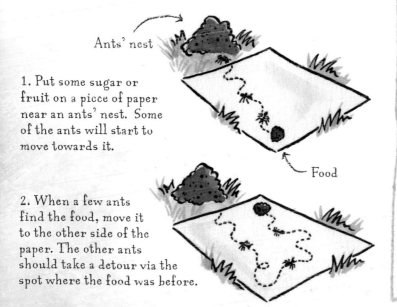

Ants' nest

1. Put some sugar or fruit on a piece of paper near an ants' nest. Some of the ants will start to move towards it.

2. When a few ants find the food, move it to the other side of the paper. The other ants should take a detour via the spot where the food was before.

Food

The arrows on the diagram show the direction of the dance.

Blending in

Insects make a tasty meal for many animals, from birds to mammals, to reptiles and other creepy-crawlies. Luckily for them, there are ways to avoid being eaten. But, for you, this can make them harder to spot.

Some insects can make themselves almost invisible. Many have colours that match their background, helping them to blend in. Others look like a part of their habitat, such as a twig, or some leaves. This disappearing trick is known as camouflage. Here are some good ones to look out for:

You could easily think that this early thorn moth caterpillar is just part of the twig.

INSECT FACT

When threatened, some types of click beetle play dead by lying on their backs, and keeping very still. This trick often works because many animals would rather eat live insects than dead ones.

If it doesn't work, the click beetle can catapult itself up to 30cm into the air to escape its attacker.

Angle shades moths look like a pile of crumpled up leaves.

This unsuspecting fly didn't see the crab spider until it was too late.

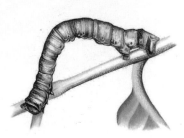

Peppered moth caterpillars look like twigs. They can be green or brown.

Comma caterpillars blend in by looking a bit like bird droppings.

Fighting back

It's easy to spot water boatmen on ponds (see page 84), but don't be tempted to pick one up. The chances are you'll be rewarded with a sharp pain as it jabs you with its pointy feeding tube, and injects you with venom.

Plenty of other insects will attack if threatened. They're armed with all sorts of weapons – from pincers to needle-sharp legs to venomous stings. Beware of bees, wasps ants, horseflies and mosquitos!

BITTER BLOOD

If you pick up a ladybird, it might leave an orange stain on your hand. This is blood from its legs. It tastes bitter to other insects and puts them off eating it. It doesn't put birds off them though!

Yum

Looking scary

Some insects use colour and markings to defend themselves. Wasps, bees and other insects that sting or taste bad are boldly coloured, to warn animals off eating them.

Puss moth caterpillars have markings on their heads that look like a scary face. If they are threatened, they pull their heads down to frighten predators away.

OFF-PUTTING INSECTS

Peacock butterflies have round markings that look like eyes, which scare off predators.

Hover flies look like dangerous wasps, with their bright stripes. In fact, they have no sting.

The caterpillar's eyes are actually at the bottom of the "face". It waves its tail around too for extra "scare factor".

Let's bee together

FANTASTIC FACT

The energy in about 30 grams of honey would give a bee enough energy to fly around the world.

A lot of bees live alone, but honey bees and bumble bees are whizzes at teamwork. They live in nests or man-made boxes called hives. Nowadays, most honey bees live in hives, looked after by beekeepers who farm them for their honey.

In each community of bees, every type or "caste" of bee has a vital job to do. There's one queen bee who lays the eggs. Male bees called drones are on hand to mate with the queen, but they don't do much else... and female worker bees do all the other jobs!

Here are the different castes of bee to spot. There are lots of different species of bumble bees and honey bees.

	Drone	Queen	Worker
	Spot these... in summer	Spot these... if you're incredibly lucky!	Spot these... from spring to autumn
Honey bees	 Drones get kicked out of the hive and die soon after mating.	 A queen can live for years, but only leaves the hive once, to mate.	 Most honey bees that you spot will be workers.
Red-tailed bumble bees	 Bumble bee drones forage alone after mating with the queen.	 Queens can be seen flying low in spring, looking for new nests.	 You might spot worker bumble bees during warm winters too.

Hard workers

Most of the bees in a honey or bumble bee colony are workers, and it's these industrious insects that give bees their reputation for being busy. Look for them in gardens, fields, parks and other flowery places. They buzz from flower to flower, collecting dusty grains called pollen and sticky nectar to feed the queen, the drones and the hungry little larvae.

This worker bee is putting nectar into the wax cells of the hive.

A cosy teapot

In spring, when bumble bee queens are looking for new homes, try leaving an old teapot in a sheltered place outside. This would be a cosy spot for the queen to nest. Make sure the pot doesn't have a grille at the bottom of the spout, so she can get in.

Put some cotton wool inside the teapot and then bury it with just a bit of the spout sticking out. Make sure you leave the lid on!

Put a bit of broken pot over the spout, so that the pot doesn't fill up with water, but leave a gap for the bee to get in and out.

BEE HELPFUL

It's getting harder for bumble bees to find the right food as there are fewer wild flowers in fields nowadays. You can help by growing their favourites in your garden or window box. Plants such as lavender, foxglove and michaelmas daisies are best.

45

*TYPES OF BLACK
GARDEN ANT*

The worker ants are about
4mm long, about half the
length of a queen.

Male ants fly out of the
nest in July and August.
After mating, they die.

The queen flies out with
the males to mate as part
of a "mating swarm". Her
wings drop off afterwards.

SPOTTER TIP
Yellow meadow ants
are often mistaken
for red ants due to
their yellow-orange
colour. If you're in
a field or a garden,
then it's probably a
yellow meadow ant
because red ants
prefer woodlands.

Red ant   Yellow
           meadow ant

Ants at home

Like honey bees, ants often live together
in big groups. Ant nests, or colonies, work
pretty much like bee hives, with the queen,
the breeding males and the female worker
ants all keeping busy at their different jobs.
The larger worker ants sometimes act as
soldiers, defending the nest and attacking
other colonies.

Ant nests can be made out of different
materials, depending on the species of ant.
Black garden ant colonies, for example,
are made up of lots of little underground
tunnels. You'll find these nests in gardens
and you can recognize them because the
mined-out earth forms a flattish mound.

Look for these in lawns, at the base of
walls, or in cracks between paving slabs.

Ants (and nests) to spot

Black garden ant
3-9mm long
Builds nests in gardens
and parks, often near
buildings. Sometimes
wanders inside looking
for food. They're actually
dark brown.

Yellow meadow ant
2-9mm long
Makes little mounds
in grassy areas. Often
forages for food
underground and farms
aphids inside its nest.

Red wood ant

5-11mm long
Builds large cone shaped
nests from twigs and
leaves in pine woods
Watch out – they can
squirt acid if you come
too close.

Red ant

3-6mm long
There are a couple of
different types of these in
Europe. They nest under
stones or in rotting
wood, where they
rear aphids for
their honeydew.

SLAVE DRIVERS

Certain species of
ants raid other ant
colonies and snatch
young ants. They
take them back to
their own colony and
raise them as slaves.
But it's not a bad life.
The "slave" ants live
just like any other
worker ant.

Turf ant

2-4mm long
Lives on heathlands
and builds nests under
stones. These nests are
mostly found in the
Southeast of England.

Jet black ant

4-5mm long
Has a heart-shaped head
and its colonies can be
found inside dead tree
stumps and in hedges,
mostly in the Southeast
of England.

Red wood ants such as
these worker ants like
sunny spots to build
their nests.

A male great diving beetle
swimming underwater

Out and about

Now you know more about watching insects, you can start to be a more hands-on spotter. This section takes you through the best ways to hunt for insects (without doing them any harm), plus how to build your own butterfly house, how to keep tabs on the snails in your garden, and all kinds of clever (but kind) experiments. You might like to put an insect diary together to keep track of your finds, too.

HUNTING KIT

You don't need a lot of equipment, but some basic kit can be very useful when you're looking for insects.

You can pop the creatures that you find in a clear jar.

Nets are great for catching flying insects.

A torch will help you find insects at night.

Use a spade or a trowel to dig for creatures in the soil.

You can sift insects out of the soil with a garden sieve.

You'll need a field guide to help you identify your finds.

Once you've caught a creature you might want to keep it for a while. Find out how to do this on pages 54-55.

Gentle insect hunting

There's nothing wrong with catching insects to get a closer look at them – so long as you handle them with care and put them back where you found them afterwards. Capturing insects gives you a chance to learn much more about their habits than you could in the wild, when they could scurry off at any moment.

Looking for signs

Insects leave all sorts of tell-tale signs behind to let you know where they've been. If you spot one of these signs, there's a good chance that the creature is still nearby.

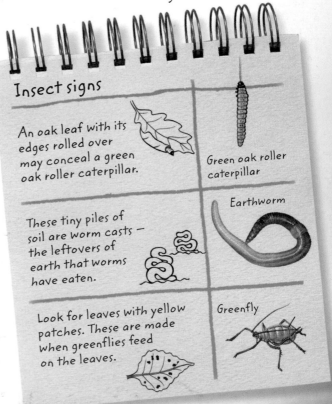

Insect signs

An oak leaf with its edges rolled over may conceal a green oak roller caterpillar.

Green oak roller caterpillar

These tiny piles of soil are worm casts – the leftovers of earth that worms have eaten.

Earthworm

Look for leaves with yellow patches. These are made when greenflies feed on the leaves.

Greenfly

Catching insects

There are all sorts of ways to catch insects. For flying insects, sneak up on them with a net. Stalk your insect slowly and quietly before you swish your net over it.

A larger net, called a sweep net, is best for scooping up insects in long grass. Long-handled pond nets make fast work of scooping up water-loving insects. Make sure you have a tray of pond water to hand to put them in. Find out more on page 83.

Up close

Once you've caught an insect, you need to put it in a container so that you can take a good look at it. A wide-necked jar with a lid will do the trick, but bug boxes are even better. These are see through cubes with a magnifying glass at one end. You can buy them in gift shops at most natural history museums.

If you don't have a bug box, use a magnifying glass to look at your catch.

HANDY HINTS

To trap an insect securely inside your net, quickly twist the handle round to double the netting over the opening.

Carefully slip a jar into the net and trap the insect between the mouth of the jar and the net.

If you don't have a net, put a piece of white cloth under a bush, and gently knock the bush with a stick. This should make a few insects drop onto the cloth.

SNAIL SNOOPING

Slow-moving creatures, such as snails, are easy to track because they don't tend to stray over long distances. One simple way to get to know the habits of snails is by marking their shells with nail polish or paint.

Each day, look for snails with marked shells in the garden. Keep notes of where you spot them. Do the same snails come back to the same place every day?

DIY SPIDERS' WEBS

If you have an old picture frame, take the back off and put it in your garden in a spot where you've seen lots of spiders. If you're lucky, a passing spider will spin its web in it.

Insect experiments

You can get to know a lot more about insects by setting little tasks for them to do, or by keeping tabs on them as they go about their business.

Underwater observations

To get a better look at underwater insects, you could make your own pond viewer using an ice cream tub and some strong cling film or a piece of hard, clear plastic that's a bit smaller than the lid of the tub.

1. Cut out the bottom of the tub.

2. Paint the outsides with black gloss paint. This will keep out extra light and help you see more clearly.

3. Cut out the middle of the lid leaving a few centimetres around the edge.

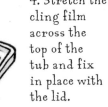

4. Stretch the cling film across the top of the tub and fix in place with the lid.

5. If you press the viewer – cling film side down – to the surface of the pond, you'll be able to see clearly into the water below.

Sugaring

You can attract moths and other insects by painting sticky mixtures onto trees. They'll be attracted to the sweet smell, and land beside the sticky area to lap up the delicious sticky goo. This is called sugaring.

1. Mix together a tin of syrup, some brown sugar and a few glugs of fruit juice. Stir it until it's evenly mixed.

2. Paint the mixture onto tree trunks or wooden posts in the late afternoon. Paint a fairly thin layer of the stuff to avoid trapping the insects.

3. You can collect the insects with a net and have a closer look before letting them go again.

This drinker moth is one of the weird and wonderful specimens you might attract.

WOODLOUSE KINGDOM

You could create a few mini habitats for woodlice in a plastic tray with deep sides. For example, you could put some moss in one corner, some twigs in another, and a few damp stones in another corner to create a shady area.

Then catch some woodlice – you can find them easily under stones – and put them in the tray. What parts of the mini-kingdom do they prefer?

FIELD TIP

When you catch an insect, keep it in a container until you get home. Note down where you found it. Was it a dry place or a damp one? Sunny or shady?

This will help you make its home-from-home more like its natural habitat.

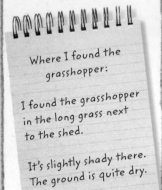

Where I found the grasshopper:

I found the grasshopper in the long grass next to the shed.

It's slightly shady there. The ground is quite dry.

OBSERVER'S TIPS

Look at your insects every day. Note down how much they eat, and describe any changes you see.

If you keep more than one type of caterpillar, see if they behave differently from one another. Do they eat or move differently?

Keeping creepy-crawlies

Any creature you catch should be kept in an environment that's as similar as possible to its natural home. A large glass jar should be fine for some, but others need a much larger space. So for them it's best to buy an aquarium. (A small one will do.)

If you found the creature in damp earth, add soil to your jar or aquarium. If it usually lives in water, fill the container with water from a pond or stream (not tap water), and put a little sand at the bottom.

Insect kit

With a few basic bits of equipment, you can keep a wide variety of insects. Once you've made a home for them, you need to feed your captives with the right food. On the page opposite, you can find some tips about what to keep which insects in, and what to give them to eat.

An aquarium

Lampshade frame

Compost

String

A large jam jar

Netting

Sand

Grasshoppers

Keep grasshoppers in an aquarium with sand in the bottom, and a cover of fine netting secured with string. Put fresh grass in every other day.

Snails

Keep snails in an aquarium with a tight-fitting lid with air holes. Put some compost at the bottom. Feed them on scraps of fresh fruit and vegetables every day.

Compost

IMPORTANT!

Keep your insects at room temperature and out of direct sunlight. Always remember to put your insects back where you found them as soon as you've finished watching them.

Dragonfly nymphs

Keep a dragonfly nymph in a large, water-filled jar covered with mesh. Scoop small pond insects into the water for it to eat.

Wire mesh

Stones and sand

Moths

A cage made from an old lampshade with netting wrapped around it will give moths a bit of room to fly.

Lampshade frame

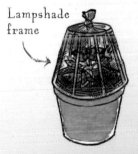

READY TO SHED

A dragonfly or damselfly nymph may shed its skin and become an adult while you're keeping it. Put an upright stick in the jar for it to cling to. If it crawls up the stick, that means it's ready to shed its skin and will do so within about an hour.

An adult damselfly emerging from the nymph's skin.

Ladybirds

Keep ladybirds in a large aquarium to give them room to fly. They eat greenfly and aphids, so find a rose shoot with these bugs on it and keep it in water in the aquarium.

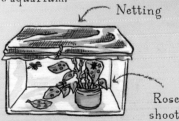

Netting

Rose shoots

Insect galls

Collect galls (see page 75) from different trees in August. Put each in its own jar, leaning the twig against the side. The insects should come out about a month later.

The old skin clings to the stick.

This cabbage white is emerging from its pupa.

Building a butterfly house

One of the most rewarding types of insects to keep are caterpillars. You will have the chance to watch the amazing transformation from caterpillar to chrysalis to butterfly (or moth).

You can make your own butterfly house with a see-through container, such as an aquarium.

1. Find a caterpillar, then pick it up gently by letting it walk onto the palm of your hand. Take the leaf that it's sitting on, too. Identify it using your field guide.

2. Put it in the container along with a handful of the same type of leaf that you found it on.

TOP TIPS

Here are some tips to help you run your butterfly house:

-Put the food plant in water so it stays fresh.

-When a caterpillar gets big it may stop eating. Don't worry: it just means it's ready to pupate.

-Check every day to see if there's enough food.

-Gently clean the cage each day, so that bug droppings don't pile up.

3. Fix some sticks upright in the box - the caterpillar will need these when it turns into a pupa.

Fix the cloth in place with tape or string.

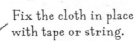

4. Put the lid on the aquarium (it should have holes so that the caterpillar can breathe) or cover it with thin cloth such as muslin.

Caring for your caterpillar

Give your caterpillar fresh food every day until it turns into a pupa. Then, just wait for the butterfly to emerge. Different breeds take different lengths of time. If you've caught a painted lady caterpillar, for example, it should take about ten days to turn into a pupa, then ten more days or so to turn into a butterfly.

Caterpillars are very fussy eaters, so don't just bung any old leaves in there. Here are examples of what some common breeds eat:

IMPORTANT

When the butterfly comes out of the pupa, have a good look at it, then return it to the place where you found the caterpillar.

Painted lady caterpillars eat thistle, mallow and hollyhocks.

The holly blue caterpillar eats holly and ivy.

Orange tip caterpillars eat the seed pods of Lady's smock.

Purple emperor caterpillars eat goat willow leaves.

Small copper caterpillars eat sorrel and dock.

Large white (also known as cabbage white) caterpillars feed on cabbage leaves.

PHOTO TIP

If you have a digital camera (or even a camera phone), take it with you when you go out spotting. Slow-moving creatures are the easiest to snap. But if you're patient and don't make too much noise, you can photograph all kinds of skittering, flying and jumping insects.

Keeping an insect diary

Keeping your own insect diary will help you remember what you've seen, and it will help you to see patterns in what insects do. As the seasons go by, you'll start to get a feel for the rhythms of the creepy-crawly lifestyle.

It's best to use a spiral-bound notebook to scribble down notes when you're out spotting. Then you can tear off the pages and stick your notes in a scrap book, or copy them into a diary.

Take photos

Label your sketch to say where you saw the creepy-crawly.

14th May

Saw a snail crawling over a rock.

22nd August

Bee on a daisy in a local farmer's field.

Saw a common blue butterfly flying low.

Saw a stag beetle near an old tree stump.

I lifted an old tree branch and found lots of woodlice.

You can draw simple sketches too.

You could trace a picture of a creepy-crawly you've spotted from a field guide.

Who, what, where?

The more you write down, draw and stick into your diary, the more useful it will be when you refer back to it. But it's always worth starting with the basics.

Jot down where you saw an insect and what it was, if you know its name. If not, describe it and try to identify it later.

Date: June 4th
Place: In the playground at school

I saw a group of black garden ants near a banana that someone dropped. I think there were about twenty of them.

Later I saw a butterfly on the playground fence. It had black wings with white spots and an orange stripe. Looked it up when I got home — it's a red admiral.

School

Red admiral butterfly

Ants eating banana

SPOTTER TIPS

*Kneel to inspect soil and grass. You'll see more than if you're standing up.

*Turn over logs and stones. Insects love to hide under these.

*Keep spotting all through the year to see different insects in different seasons.

*Join a conservation group to get spotter advice and help save insects!

Insects all around you

You don't need to go far from your own front door to spot insects. Whether you're in a garden, in the park, or just walking down the road, they'll never be far away. Some love to nestle in piles of rotting wood, while others thrive on flowers or in ponds. Some even make their homes indoors... and all kinds of creatures like a nice thick compost heap.

Common wasps buzzing around an ivy plant in flower

BUILD A MINI GARDEN

You can watch insects from the comfort of your room by creating a window box. Fill plant pots with soil and plant flower seeds in them (the packets will tell you which time of year is best). Place the pots on your windowsill. When the flowers bloom, they will attract all kinds of insects.

Indoors and outdoors

Gardens are a spotter's paradise because they can contain so many different mini-habitats (also called micro-habitats.) And the more mini-habitats in a garden, the more types of creeping, flying, burrowing and scampering creatures you can spot. But if you don't have a garden, there are insects to spot indoors too.

Mulch munchers

A compost heap or bin is like a luxury hotel for creepy-crawlies, and they're very helpful guests. As they feed on the plants and scraps of food, they help break them down into a nutrient-rich mush, which can be used to make gardens grow better. Not all insects eat scraps, though. Some prefer to snack on their fellow guests.

Here are some of the creatures you'll find in compost.

HEAP TIP

Here are some of the things you can put on a compost heap:

- Twigs and branches
- Shredded cardboard
- Teabags
- Crushed eggshells
- Clean pet bedding, such as sawdust
- Weeds
- Leaves
- Vegetable peelings

Rove beetle

Common earwig

Earthworm

Slug

Woodlouse

Ants

Pollinating flowers

You'll often see insects feeding on flowers, but they're not just helping themselves, they're helping the flowers too.

When insects crawl into flowering plants, they get dusted with grains of pollen. For many plants to reproduce, pollen has to be carried to another plant. As the insects fly away, they take pollen with them, and the grains rub off on the next flower they land on. This is called pollination.

This bee is covered with pollen that it's collected from inside this crocus flower.

Some bees, such as this buff-tailed bumblebee, collect lots of pollen on their back legs.

The bee takes some of this back to its nest for food, but a lot rubs off inside the next flower.

House guests

Like it or not, you're probably sharing your home with a whole host of creatures. Moths, spiders, flies and crane flies are often found indoors where it's warm and dry. Bees, butterflies and ladybirds may also creep inside to hibernate during the cold winter.

Some insects are lured in by the possibility of a feast. Mosquitos feed on blood. So if you hear a high, whining noise on a summer's night, you may have a hungry guest...

SAVE A SPIDER

If you find a spider that's fallen into the bath, it won't be able to get out on its own because the sides are too slippery. Lift it out gently by allowing it to crawl onto your hand, or tie a piece of string to a tap so that it can climb out.

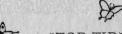

TOP TIP

To get loads of
different types of
creatures in your
garden, create
different types
of habitats – for
example, a wet area,
a dry, sunny area
and a grassy area.

An insect garden

If you've got a garden there's a lot you can do
to encourage many more insects to live there.
On these pages you can find some suggestions
for turning a garden into insect heaven. One
thing's for sure, they prefer messy gardens to
tidy ones!

The more types of flowers
there are, the more varied
insect visitors there will be.

USEFUL INSECTS

Instead of using
chemicals to protect
your plants from
plant-eating insects,
encourage creatures
that eat insect-pests.

It's much better
for the environment
to use natural pest
controllers like
these, rather than
chemicals, which
can kill other
insects – and
other animals too.

Small tortoiseshell
butterfly

Hover flies and
many butterflies
love lavender.

Garden spider

A centipede

Violet ground
beetle

64

If you have a wild patch in your garden, it'll attract more insects. Let the grass grow long, and sow some wild flower seeds.

A compost bin will attract all sorts of creatures, including worms, woodlice, fly larvae and fruit flies.

Other weeds may attract insects too. Many butterflies love nettles.

Ponds attract lots of water-loving insects.

A millipede

A woodlouse

If you are lucky, a stag beetle may lay its eggs on a rotting tree stump.

TO BUILD A POND

If you have a pond, you can attract even more insects.

1. Dig a hole somewhere that gets equal amounts of sun and shade. Give it gently sloping sides and shallow edges.

2. Line the hole with sand, some plastic sheeting and a pond liner from a garden centre.

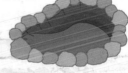

3. Fill the pond with water, and leave it to settle for a few days. Then weigh down the edges of the liner with stones.

4. Put plants, such as bullrushes and water irises, in the pond, and grass on its banks. These will act as insect homes.

FOOL A WORM

In your local park, try a few tricks to coax worms to the surface. Tap the ground with sticks to imitate the sound of raindrops. Or try pouring water on the ground and wait for the worms to pop out of the soil. You'll need to wait for a few minutes while they crawl up through the soil.

Towns and parks

Take a walk around your local town and see what insects you can spot in the streets and parks. Peer closely at brick walls, especially in the spaces between bricks and at the bottom of walls, where some ants and bees like to make their homes. Garden hedges can be very popular hiding places. Look for privet hawk moths and privet hawk moth caterpillars in privet hedges.

In your local park, look closely at the trees, especially at the gaps in the bark and any hollow bits where beetles often lurk. If there's a pond, stop and watch for flies, dragonflies and damselflies flitting over the surface. Look in the reeds beside the water and the trees hanging over it too.

Yellow brimstone butterfly

Peacock butterfly

Blow fly

Caddisfly

Canal dwellers

Canals are good places to see water insects. Look out for damselflies and dragonflies, such as the blue-tailed damselfly, which is often found on plants near canals and ditches. The magnificent emperor dragonfly also flies near canals. But be very careful near the water's edge, and don't go without an adult.

OTHER TOWN HABITATS

Look for insects in:

- Grassy churchyards
- Old mossy walls
- The edges of your school sports field
- Allotments
- Greenhouses and other outside buildings

Emperor dragonfly

Blue tailed damselfly

Indoor zoo

Don't forget to look inside buildings, such as sheds and greenhouses. Spiders love to build their webs in the corners of rooms and you'll often see them in places that haven't been dusted for a while. If you look inside a shed, you'll have a good chance of seeing quite a few webs that haven't been disturbed.

LOFTS AND CELLARS

Lots of insects like to hide away in the places that humans don't often go. Woodlice love nice damp cellars, while wasps often build their paper nests in attics. If you see a lot of wasps in your house, you might have a nest tucked away in the rafters.

Twenty two-spot ladybird

Seven-spot ladybird

Black and yellow crane fly

Privet hawk moth caterpillar

FANTASTIC FACT
Adult sexton beetles work in pairs to bury the remains of small animals. The female then lays eggs nearby, and the adults stick around to protect their young. You can spot sexton beetles in open grassy areas.

1. The adults creep underneath the dead animal and start to dig away the soil.

2. The animal gradually sinks down into the earth until it's completely buried. This takes about eight hours.

Creatures to spot

All the animals on these pages should be easy to spot in a garden, or park.

Carefully lift large rocks and you are guaranteed to find a whole host of creatures, such as woodlice and millipedes. You might find insects that feed on sap on the underside of leaves. Try looking amongst fallen leaves for beetles and earwigs.

Zebra spider
5-7mm long
This meat-eating spider has two very large, keen-sighted eyes to help it spot its prey. It can be found on walls, fences and plants on a sunny day.

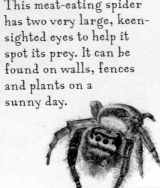

Hover fly
10-15mm long
Cannot sting, despite looking a little like bees and wasps. Adult feeds on nectar. Larvae eat aphids and other sap-sucking insects.

Pill millipede
20mm long
Looks similar to a woodlouse, but has 17-19 pairs of legs. (Woodlice have only 7 pairs.) Curls up into a ball when threatened.

Greenfly
2-3mm long
A type of aphid. Females can have babies without a male, and can give birth to live young. Feeds on plant sap, and can do a lot of damage in gardens.

Small tortoiseshell

25mm wingspan
One of Europe's most common butterflies to spot in the garden. Can be found on nettles. Caterpillars are black and yellow.

Common froghopper

6mm long
Young feed on plants and cover themselves in white froth, known as cuckoo spit. This protects them from predators. Adult can jump up to 50cm if threatened.

Brimstone butterfly

30mm wingspan
Can be found in hedges, and feeds on buckthorn. Hibernates in winter in ivy and other evergreens. One of the first butterflies to appear in spring.

Cinnabar moth

40-45mm wingspan
Flies during the day as well as at night. Hairy black and gold caterpillars feed on ragwort and groundsel.

Seven-spot ladybird

5-9mm long
Feeds on small soft insects, especially aphids. Often found near wood ant nests, which feed off the sticky liquid that aphids make.

Green lacewing

15mm long
Feeds on aphids, and is attracted to light. May hibernate in the winter in houses. Larvae cover their bodies with dead aphids to disguise themselves.

Lily beetle

6-8mm long
Feeds on lily plants. Larvae are orangey-red, but coat themselves with their black poo, and look a bit like bird droppings.

Leafcutter bee

10-11mm long
Cuts semi-circular holes in the edges of leaves from plants such as roses and fuschias. Uses the leaf-clippings to make nest walls.

Green shield bug

14mm long
Bright green in spring and summer, but bronze in the autumn. Hibernates in the winter. Feeds on plant sap.

BUILD A LIGHT TRAP

Many nocturnal animals are attracted to light.

You can make a simple light trap to get a closer look at them.

At night, hang a white sheet from the branches of a tree or on a bush. Shine a bright light (the bigger, the better) on the sheet. Insects will soon be drawn to it.

Write down what you find in your insect diary.

28th June, evening, in the garden

I saw... six European black slugs munching on some cabbages.

... two ghost moths fluttering over the lawn at dusk.

...and a herald moth landed on the kitchen window drawn to the light.

In the dark

If you take a torch outside after dark, you might be surprised how many creatures you can spot – from fluttering, furry moths, to scurrying, woodlice, to slow-moving slimy slugs. In fact, many insects only come out at night. They are known as nocturnal insects. Some of the creatures you find in your house like the dark, too. Spiders, moths, silverfish, cockroaches all like to lurk in dark nooks and corners.

This spectacular canary shouldered thorn moth is found in woods at night.

Creatures to spot

Garden snail
25-30mm across

Leaves a silvery trail of mucus, and feeds on plants. Withdraws into its shell when threatened.

Silverfish
up to 12mm long

Lives mainly in dark, damp places, indoors. Can run very fast and feeds on mould and the glue that holds books together.

House spider
10-12mm long

Found in gardens and homes, often in baths. Feeds on creepy-crawlies such as earwigs, beetles and cockroaches.

Pill woodlouse
11mm long

Found in damp places such as compost heaps and under stones. Feeds on rotting plants and its own droppings. Rolls up into a ball when threatened.

European black slug
up to 150mm long

Like snails, produces slimy mucus, leaving a silvery trail wherever it goes. When threatened, it pulls its body up into a ball.

Devil's coach-horse beetle
25-30mm long

Hunts at night for slugs, worms and woodlice. When threatened, it raises its tail. Has a painful bite.

Ghost moth
50-60mm wingspan

Males hovers over open ground to attract females. Female has yellow wings.

Common earwig
10-15mm long

The male has wings, but rarely flies. Its pincers are slightly more curved than the female's. Can be found in damp cool places in gardens.

Glow worm
15-20mm long

The female's tail glows in the dark to attract males. The male has wings and a fluttering moth-like flight.

UNDERGROUND PESTS

Vine weevil larvae nibble away at the roots of plants, causing the plants to wither and die. They are especially fond of plants in pots. Look out for tell-tale signs – leaves suddenly turning yellow and wilting. You can gently tip the plant out to look for the grubs.

In the ground

If you dig up a spadeful of earth, the chances are it will be teeming with insect life. It's not just worms that live in the ground.

Hundreds of thousands of tiny animals live down below the surface where they can find food, shelter and are hidden from many predators – everything they need to survive.

In and out

Many creatures spend their larval stage underground and only come up to live above ground when they are adults. If you are on sandy soil, look carefully for tiny holes in the ground. These could be the entrances to beetle larvae burrows. Tiger beetle larvae dig a burrow, then wait near its mouth to ambush any bugs that pass by. If you keep very quiet and still, you may see the larvae pop up for a feast.

This centipede lives under stones and burrows down into the soil, looking for prey.

Creatures to spot

Earthworm
90-300mm
Lives in the soil up to 2m down, but comes up to the surface to mate, or when it's raining. Feeds on rotting vegetation. Leaves behind squiggly piles of digested food, known as worm casts.

Mole cricket
38-42mm
Spends its time tunnelling underground, but swarms on warm evenings in mainland Europe. Males make purring sounds at the entrances to their burrows. Prefers moist sand and mud.

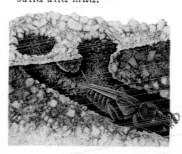

Mining bee
10-15mm
Solitary bee that digs down deep into soft soil to build a nest, where it lays eggs, and stores pollen and nectar for its larvae. Often digs in lawns, leaving tell-tale little piles of soil.

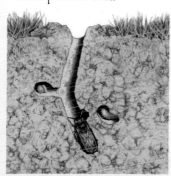

Purse web spider
12-16mm
Digs a burrow about 20cm down into the ground and lines it with silk. The last 9cm of silk pokes out above the ground and looks a little like the inflated finger of a rubber glove.

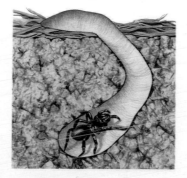

MAKE A WORMERY

You can make a worm home and see for yourself what worms get up to underground.

Leave a 5cm space at the top

1. Put alternate layers of sand (2cm deep) and soil (5cm deep) in a glass jar. Dig up some worms and put them in the jar.

2. Add vegetable peel, then put a lid, with holes in it, on the jar. Cover the jar with a dark cloth, and leave it for two weeks before you look to see what the worms are doing.
   They will have mixed up the soil and made tunnels.

*FANTASTIC
FACT*

New Zealand
flatworms feed on
earthworms. They
eat them by lying
on top of them and
injecting them with
chemicals from
their bodies. The
chemicals liquidize
the insides of the
earthworm, and the
flatworm then sucks
up the liquid.

Alien invaders

There are lots of types of animals in northern Europe that originally came from elsewhere. Some of them arrive by hitching a lift – in crates of food brought from other parts of the world, or among the roots of plants.

Others have moved north, as the weather has become warmer. Some of these alien invaders can be bad news for native species.

Wasp spiders originally came from southern Europe, but they have been seen as far north as Sweden.

Creatures to spot

Wasp spider
4-15mm long
Origin: southern Europe
Feeds on small insects. Its web has a distinctive zig zag of white silk in it. Can be found in long grass.

Girdled snail
14mm long
Origin: Mediterranean
First spotted in the UK in 1950. Feeds on almost any vegetation. Can be found in hedges and gardens, in shady places.

False widow spider
7-14mm long
Origin: Canary Islands
Found in houses and outbuildings, feeding on flies and small insects. May give a painful bite if provoked.

Harlequin ladybird
7-8mm long
Origin: Asia
Varies in appearance, but the most common are orange with 15-21 black spots, and red with 2 or 4 orange or black spots. Eats native ladybirds.

Hummingbird hawk moth
40-50mm wingspan
Origin: Mediterranean, central Asia and Japan
Feeds on the nectar of flowers, hovering above them like a hummingbird.

Madeira bark louse
5mm long
Origin: Madeira and the Canary Islands
A type of bark fly, lives on the bark of trees and shrubs, feeding on algae and lichen. First spotted in southern England in 2006.

New Zealand flatworm
4-11mm long
Origin: New Zealand
Feeds on native worms. Found in cool, damp places, often under pots, logs and stones. Has black, 1cm long eggs.

Asian hornet
76mm wingspan
Origin: Asia
Aggressive wasp that arrived in France in 2004. Feeds on insects, including honey bees. Has a very painful sting.

Colorado beetle
10-12mm long
Origin: North America
Widespread throughout mainland Europe, but not the UK. Damages potatoes. You should tell the police if you see one.

Wood ant workers
defending their nest

Insect habitats

Insects can live almost anywhere, but you'll find different kinds of insect in different types of habitat. In a woodland glade, you might find hordes of busy wood ants, scurrying about on the forest floor, while in a boggy area, you can spot darting dragonflies.

In this section, you can find out about places you can go to spot insects, from rolling, flowery heaths to slow-flowing streams.

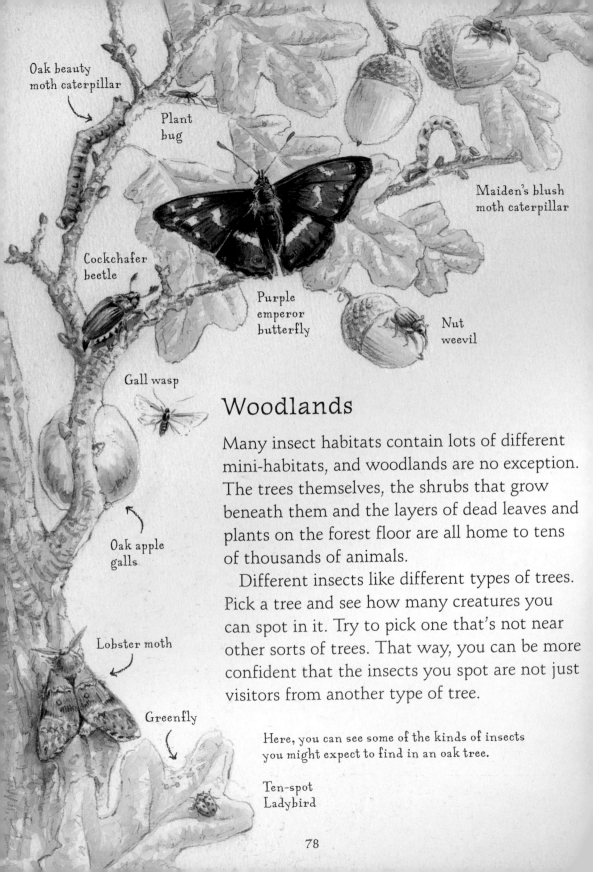

Oak beauty
moth caterpillar

Plant
bug

Maiden's blush
moth caterpillar

Cockchafer
beetle

Purple
emperor
butterfly

Nut
weevil

Gall wasp

Oak apple
galls

Lobster moth

Greenfly

Ten-spot
Ladybird

Woodlands

Many insect habitats contain lots of different mini-habitats, and woodlands are no exception. The trees themselves, the shrubs that grow beneath them and the layers of dead leaves and plants on the forest floor are all home to tens of thousands of animals.

Different insects like different types of trees. Pick a tree and see how many creatures you can spot in it. Try to pick one that's not near other sorts of trees. That way, you can be more confident that the insects you spot are not just visitors from another type of tree.

Here, you can see some of the kinds of insects you might expect to find in an oak tree.

Shrubs and flowers

You'll find loads of insects in amongst the shrubs in woods. Hundreds of kinds of beetles live there. Some feed off leaves, sucking out sap or just munching on them, while others hunt other small creatures. You can also spot wasps, crickets and grasshoppers.

Nearer the ground, look out for hover flies, moths and butterflies. You're most likely to find them in flowery areas, in places where there is not too much shade, or in sunny clearings, feeding on grasses.

ROTTEN HOMES

Trees don't stop giving shelter to animals even when they're dead.

Fungi and tiny organisms rot down the wood, and insects such as stag beetle larvae feed off them. A dead and decaying tree can be home to as many as 1,800 species.

Living in litter

Gently scrape back some of the fallen leaves that lie on the woodland's floor and you'll see dozens of little creatures scurrying for cover.

Mites, springtails, millipedes and beetles all make their home in the wood's leafy litter. Some feed on the rotten plant matter, while others are bug-eating predators.

Violet ground beetles forage for woodlice and slugs in the litter.

SPOTTING TIP

If you are in an oak wood, look out for small round balls on oak trees. These are made by oak apple gall-wasps. They each contain a gall-wasp larva.

Creatures to spot

Some insects prefer certain types of trees. So, knowing what sort of tree you are looking at will help you to identify the insects that are in it. Don't forget to look in all the different "layers" of the wood – in the trees, among the shrubs and on the ground, under dead leaves and stones. Here are some common forest-dwelling creatures to spot.

Horse fly
20-25mm long
Female sucks blood from animals, including people. Male feeds on nectar. Can be found on the outskirts of woods near damp meadows.

Forest bug
11-14mm long
A large type of shield bug, common on oak and fruit trees. Feeds on leaf sap and sometimes other insects.

Horned treehopper
9-10mm long
Found on tree branches and low vegetation, such as bracken, in clearings. Feeds on oak leaves and other plants.

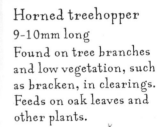

Poplar hawk moth
70-90mm wingspan
Holds its hind wings above its forewings when resting, making it look like a crumpled leaf. Larvae feed on willow and poplar trees.

Stag beetle
35-50mm long
Feeds on sap, and lays eggs in rotten wood. May be seen flying in the late afternoon or early evening. Males fight each other with their antler-like jaws.

Birch sawfly
20-23mm long
Larvae feed on birch trees in late summer. They make a large oval cocoon and emerge as adults in the spring.

Wood white butterfly

40-42mm wingspan

Lives in shady areas, feeding on woodland flowers, such as yellow vetch. When not feeding, flutters just above the flowers.

Crane fly

65mm wingspan

Rests with its wings wide apart. Has very fragile legs that easily break off when it's handled. Prefers damp woodland.

Longhorn beetle

14-20mm long

Adults feed on pollen and can be found on flowers such as hogweed and wild rose. Larvae live in rotting tree stumps.

Hornet

20-35mm wingspan

Nests in hollow tree trunks, feeding its grubs on other insects, such as butterflies. If threatened, whole nest may swarm.

Purple emperor butterfly

76-84mm wingspan

Lives in treetops, but you might see males when they come down to the ground to drink from puddles. Prefers oak woods.

Violet ground beetle

30-35mm long

Hunts at night, but can be found under stones, logs and leaves during the day. Adults and larvae eat other insects and worms.

Crab spider

3-11mm long

Lies in wait in yellow and white flowers for pollinating insects such as bees and butterflies. Camouflages itself by changing colour.

Lobster moth

40-70mm wingspan

So-called because the caterpillar looks a little like a lobster. Male is attracted to light. Caterpillars often eat each other.

Other woodland minibeasts to spot:

Common earwig (p.71)

Greenfly (p.68)

Harlequin ladybird (p.75)

Hover fly (p.68)

Green lacewing (p.69)

Pill woodlouse (p.71)

Small tortoiseshell (p.69)

Wolf spider (p.87)

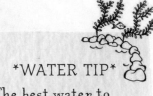

WATER TIP

The best water to
find insects in is
clear, clean water,
with plants growing
in it, but little
green algae. Plants
put oxygen into the
water and provide
shelter for insects.
Water in open
sunny areas has
the most creepy-
crawlies in it.

Ponds, lakes and streams

Ponds, lakes, rivers and streams teem with
life and provide perfect homes for countless
little creatures. Different animals like to live in
different watery habitats.

Some prefer the surface of a weedy pond,
while others like nothing better than to skulk
on the muddy bottom of a slow-moving
stream. In fact, most prefer slow-flowing or
still water. But even in fast-flowing streams
and rivers there'll be plenty to spot.

Underwater living

Many insects spend the first part of their
lives living underwater, as larvae or nymphs.
Some can breathe underwater using gills. As
they don't need to come up to the surface,
they can be tricky to spot. But others have
to come up for air, so you may see them just
above the surface. The best times to spot
larvae are spring and summer.

This great diving beetle
larva has to go to the
surface of the water to
breathe and to pupate.

Pond dipping

The best way to observe insects is to get really close-up. This can be tricky with pond-loving insects. You may need to scoop them up with a pond net to get a closer look.

You will need:
A deep, wide container (such as a cat litter tray or a big bucket) filled with pond water, a bug box (or a glass jar) and a magnifying glass, a pond net and a spoon.

1. Sweep your net through the pond, skimming the surface, and empty the net into the container.

2. Put some more pond water into the jar, and transfer the insects into it, using the spoon.

3. Take a good look at your catch, using the bug box or the magnifying glass. Note down what you see.

When you've examined all your finds, carefully put them back in the water. Then you can try again. This time sweep your net deeper to look for different creatures.

KEEP SAFE!

When you are hunting insects near water, there are a few rules you must stick to:

- Don't go into the water.

- Don't lean out over the edge of the pond.

- Don't use stones or logs as stepping stones – they may move.

- Be careful near the edge, in case it gives way.

- Always go with an adult.

SAFE AND SOUND

Caddisfly larvae can make silky threads, which they use to stick bits of stone and shells together, to make a protective "house". When threatened, they quickly nip inside it.

Water spiders live underwater. But they need air to breathe.

They build underwater nests, then collect air bubbles from the surface.

They release the bubbles into the nest, and lie in wait there for prey.

Creatures to spot

Here are some pictures to help you identify insects that live on or near water. Find out what kind of water you are about to visit – slow, fast-flowing, or still – then look at this guide, to find out what you can expect to see. Also look at the vegetation at the water's side. You never know what might be lurking there.

Water boatman
15mm long
Rests under the water or clings to plants in weedy ponds and slow-moving water. Courting males rub their front legs together to make a noise.

Water spider
8-15mm long
Covered with hairs in which it traps air bubbles from the surface. These give it a silvery sheen when it swims.

Common pond skater
8-10mm long
Skims over the surface of still and slow-moving water. Uses front legs to scoop up insects for food. Its body is covered with water-repellent hairs.

Whirligig beetle
3-25mm long
Found in large numbers on the surface of ponds and streams. Paddles around rapidly in circles looking for prey. Lays eggs under leaves on land.

Medicinal leech
50-100mm
Lives in shallow muddy pools, and feeds off the blood of animals. Latches onto an animal with its strong jaws and sucks the blood. Drops off the animal when it's full.

Giant diving beetle
25-35mm
Still-water insect, preferring weedy ponds. Dives down to the bottom to hunt for small fish, frogs and insects. Has distinctive suction pads on front legs.

Water flea
0.1-3mm long
Not really a flea, but a crustacean. Swims with a jerky movement. Can live in fresh or seawater. Is see-through which means you can see its internal organs.

Water stick insect
30-35mm
Found in still water crawling among vegetation. Has a long, pointy breathing tube for when it's underwater. Hard to spot because it's well camouflaged.

Great pond snail
45-60mm
Found in slow-moving or still water. Lives on the bottom, but can be seen floating upside down just under the surface when it comes up for air.

Mosquito
6-7mm
Found in or near any freshwater, from ponds and streams to water-filled ditches and puddles. Adults suck the blood of animals, and can spread disease.

Northern caddisfly
7-25mm
Can be found wherever there is freshwater. Larvae live on the bottoms of ponds and streams.

Water scorpion
20-35mm
Lurks in weeds in ponds grabbing insects and tadpoles with pincer-like legs. When underwater, breathes through a snorkel-like tube at the end of its body.

Common blue damselfly
35-40mm wingspan
Lives in vegetation near water. Female has a green and black spine. Makes slits in the stems of plants, just beneath the water, and lays eggs in them.

Silver studded blue
butterflies only live on
heathland in the UK.

Heathland

Heathlands are covered with low-growing plants, such as heather and bracken, with wet, boggy areas. They contain a whole host of mini-habitats where many different types of insects thrive. Heaths tend to be warm, which suits most insects. They usually have sandy soil too, which is ideal for burrowing creatures. Heathlands are home to many rare species, some of which you can only find there.

Look for different
creatures in different
mini-habitats.

Minotaur beetle on
sheep droppings

Heather

Emperor moth

Boggy
area

Dragonfly

Sandy soil

Wolf spider

Moorland clouded
butterfly

Hornet
robber fly

Sand
digger
wasp

Bilberry bushes

Creatures to spot

Grayling butterfly
56-61mm wingspan
Feeds on thistle nectar.
When the adult settles,
it folds its wings,
tucking its small orange
wings under its larger
brown ones.

Sand digger wasp
20mm long
Digs tunnels in sand in
which it lays eggs. Can
be seen hovering near
the entrance to a newly
dug burrow.

Emperor moth
55-70mm wingspan
Males fly around in the
day looking for females.
Females come out at dusk
to lay eggs. Caterpillar
feeds on heather. Adults
do not feed.

Heath assassin bug
9-12mm long
Can have long or short
wings. Chases and pounces
on other insects and small
spiders, then eats them.
Squeaks loudly when
handled.

Potter wasp
12-14mm long
Female makes a vase-
shaped nest out of sand
and clay, which she fills
with caterpillars, before
laying a single egg in it.

Wolf spider
9-12mm long
Hunts and eats small
insects. Female carries
her eggs around with
her. After they hatch,
she carries her young
for about a week.

Green hairstreak butterfly
31-34mm wingspan
Feeds on bilberry,
buckthorn and
gorse. Female
often lays eggs on
plants growing
on ant hills.

Moorland clouded yellow butterfly
53-55 wingspan
Fast-flying butterfly
that rarely rests for long.
Feeds on bilberry and
bog bilberry flowers.
Found in mainland Europe.

Minotaur beetle
12-20mm long
A type of dung beetle.
Males fight with "horns"
to win females. Often
found on rabbit and
sheep droppings.

MAKE A MINI-MARSH

1. Dig a shallow hole and line it as you would if you were making a pond. (See page 65.)

2. Put a layer of soil in it and plant water-loving plants, such as marsh marigolds, snake's head fritillaries and irises.

3. Fill your bog with rain water, or tap water that's been left to stand for a few days.

Wetlands

Wetlands are large, open places with stretches of shallow, still water and plenty of plants. Bogs, marshes, fens and shallow lakes are all wetlands, and you'll find many of them on heaths. Wetlands are fantastic places to spot all kinds of insects – particularly dragonflies and damselflies, which lay their eggs on the water or on plants nearby.

Like heath insects, some wetland insects can only be found in wetlands. As people drain wetlands to build and farm on them, some of these creatures are becoming increasingly rare.

Black tailed skimmer dragonflies prefer open water, with bare, dry patches where they can rest.

Creatures to spot

Mayfly

40mm long

Adult only lives from a few hours to a day, and doesn't feed. Nymph spends a year or two under water.

Emperor dragonfly

105mm wingspan

Seen over large stretches of still water. Adult catches flies in flight, which it often takes to nearby grassland to eat.

Great ramshorn snail

Up to 30mm long

Common snail that lives in stagnant water. Can breath underwater, but comes up for air from time to time.

Ruddy darter

35mm wingspan

A fast-flying damselfly. Females are smaller than males and have golden yellow bodies.

Bulrush wainscot moth

45-50mm wingspan

Can be seen in late summer near reed beds. Larvae feed on the pith inside reedmace stems.

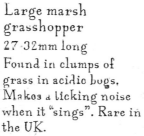

Golden-ringed dragonfly

90mm wingspan

Found near bogs and slow-flowing streams. When not flying, can be found hanging from tree branches.

China-mark moth

30mm wingspan

Lays its eggs on floating leaves. Larvae hibernate and pupate in cases they make from pieces of leaf.

Large marsh grasshopper

27-32mm long

Found in clumps of grass in acidic bogs. Makes a ticking noise when it "sings". Rare in the UK.

Other wetland animals to spot:

Crane fly (p.81)

Common blue damselfly (p.85)

Horse fly (p.80)

Medicinal leech (p.85)

Mosquito (p.85)

Northern caddisfly (p.85)

Water boatman (p.84)

CREEPY-CRAWLY COUNT

Make a 25x25cm square by winding wire around four sticks. Take it to a meadow and put it on the grass. How many minibeasts can you spot inside it?

To find out roughly how many insects live in the whole meadow, multiply the number of minibeasts you find in your patch by the area of the meadow (its width times its length). Then multiply this number by 16.

Meadow's area is its width times its length. So, if the meadow is 20x20m, its area is 400^2m.

I have found 30 insects in my patch, so there are about 30x 400x16 insects (equals 192,000) in the meadow.

Flowery grassland

Long, grassy meadows throng with life. Four square kilometres may contain as many as 2.25 million spiders. Mites and woodlice find shelter and food on the ground; higher up, caterpillars feed on leaves and stems; while, at the top, butterflies and other flying insects feed on the flowers.

The best meadows to look in are ones that are not regularly mown, as cutting the grass destroys some insect homes. Warm meadows that are surrounded by other insect habitats, such as woods, are also likely to have more insects in them.

Marbled white butterflies feed on the flowers of plants, such as thistles and knapweed.

Creatures to spot

Meadow brown butterfly

50-55mm wingspan
Can be seen in dull weather as well as on sunny days. Male makes an unpleasant scent.

Dor beetle

16-24mm long
A large type of dung beetle. Can be found crawling along the ground. Underside often infested with mites.

Gate keeper butterfly

40-46mm wingspan
Basks in sunshine on the edges of meadows, especially in hedges. Feeds on blackberry flowers.

Click beetle

14-18mm long
Can jerk themselves up into the air with a loud click if they are overturned. Larvae eat and damage crops.

Large skipper butterfly

30-32mm wingspan
Fast flying butterfly that can also be seen basking in the sun. Male jealously guards the area where it feeds, dive bombing any other butterflies that get too close.

Scarlet-tipped flower beetle

7-10mm long
Feeds on pollen and can be found in buttercup flowerheads. Blows up scarlet sacs on its underside when alarmed.

Oil beetle

15-30mm long
Lays its eggs on flowers. Larvae jump on passing bees and hitch a lift to their hive, where they feed on the bees' eggs, pollen and nectar.

Marbled white butterfly

58-58mm wingspan
Feeds on flowers such as thistles. Common in southern England and mainland Europe.

Bombardier beetle

7-10mm long
Found in dry grassland. Shoots a hot, acidic liquid out of its rear end when alarmed. Common in continental Europe, but less so in the UK.

Glossary

Here are some of the words in the book you might not know. Any word in *italics* is defined elsewhere in the glossary.

antennae "Feelers" attached to some creatures' heads. Insects can smell with their antennae, as well as feel with them.

Arachnida A *class* of animals that includes spiders.

camouflage A way of blending into the background that makes an insect hard to see.

chrysalis A butterfly *pupa*.

class A word used by scientists to describe a large group of animals, such as *Arachnida*.

Clitellata A *class* of animals that include worms and leeches.

compound eye An eye that is made up of lots of different light-gathering parts.

Crustacea A *class* of animals that includes woodlice and many water-dwelling creatures.

drone Male bee that mates with the *queen bee*.

exoskeleton The hard case around an insect's body.

field guide A book for identifying animals.

Gastropoda A *class* of animals that includes slugs, snails and whelks.

gill An organ that allows an animal to breathe underwater.

habitat A type of place where a group of animals or plants live.

hermaphrodite An animal that has both male and female body parts.

hibernation Spending long periods of time asleep during the winter.

hive A man-made home for a colony of honey bees.

larva A young insect that looks totally different to the adult. Larvae undergo *metamorphosis* to become adults.

metamorphosis The dramatic transformation that many young insects go through to become adults.

Myriapoda A *class* of animals that includes millipedes and centipedes. Myriapods have lots of legs.

nectar A sugary liquid that's produced by flowers.

nymph A young insect that looks similar to the adult.

order A group of animals, smaller than a *class*, such as beetles.

pollen Dusty grains found in flower heads. Plants use these for reproduction.

pollination The transfer of *pollen* from one plant to another to enable reproduction.

proboscis A long tube-like tongue which butterflies have. They use it to suck up *nectar*.

proleg A leg-like bump on a caterpillar. The caterpillar uses these, along with its real legs, to move.

pupa A special case that protects an insect when it is undergoing *metamorphosis*.

pupate To turn into a *pupa*.

queen bee A female bee that lays eggs. Honey bees only have one queen in each *hive*.

species A specific type of animal or plant.

spiderling A young spider.

wetlands Open areas of shallow water or water-logged ground with lots of plants.

worker bee A bee that collects *nectar* and *pollen* and does all the work in any *hive* or nest.

worm cast The digested remains of food eaten by worms.

A buff-tailed bumble
bee gathering pollen
from a hebe bush

Index

Acknowledgements

Every effort has been made to trace the copyright holders of material in this book. If any rights have been omitted, the publishers offer to rectify this in any subsequent editions following notification. The publishers are grateful to the following organizations and individuals for their permission to reproduce material

(t = top, m = middle, b = bottom, l = left, r = right):

Cover © Martin Ruegner/Masterfile www.masterfile.com; **p1** © Kim Taylor/naturepl.com; **p2–3** © Ross Hoddinott/naturepl.com; **p4–5** © Lucky Look/Alamy; **p6–7** © Andy Sands/naturepl.com; **p8** (t) © Warren Photographic; **p9** (b) © SCOTT CAMAZINE/SCIENCE PHOTO LIBRARY; **p15** (m) © Andrew Darrington/Alamy; **p16** (tl) © Andrew Darrington/Alamy; **p17** (mr) © Robert Pickett/CORBIS; **p22** (bl) © Holt Studios International Ltd/Alamy; **p23** (b) © Warren Photographic; **p23** (m) © imagebroker/Alamy; **p24–25** © Jef Meul/Foto Natura/Minden Pictures/Getty Images; **p26** (m) © Jupiterimages; **p27 (tr)** © Andrew Darrington/Alamy; **p28** (tl) © Andreas Lander/dpa/Corbis; **p31** (tr) © Steve Hopkin/ardea.com; **p32** (b) © Fritz Rauschenbach/zefa/Corbis; **p33** (tr) © Premaphotos/Alamy; **p34** © South West Images Scotland/Alamy; **p35** © blickwinkel/Alamy; **p36** (tl) © blickwinkel/Alamy; **p36** (b) © David Boag/Alamy; **p39** (br) © Andrew Darrington/Alamy; **p40** (b) © NHPA/STEPHEN DALTON; **p40** (tl) © Jason Gallier/Alamy; **p42** (tl) © Andrew Darrington/Alamy; **p43** (b) © INGO ARNDT/FOTO NATURA/Minden Pictures/FLPA; **p45** (tr) © Papilio/Alamy; **p47** (b) © Jeffrey Jackson/Alamy; **p48–49** © Andy Sands/naturepl.com; **p51** (b) © Botanica/Oxford Scientific; **p53** (b) © Warren Photographic; **p55** (br) © Joe McDonald/CORBIS; **p57** (t) © Nature Picture Library/Alamy; **p60–61** © Kim Taylor/naturepl.com; **p63 (tr)** © Pixonnet.com/Alamy; **p70** (b) © David Forster/Alamy; **p72** (b) © Harold Taylor/Oxford Scientific; **p74** © Junior Bildarchiv/Alamy; **p76–77** © Warren Photographic; **p79** (br) © Simon Colmer and Abby Rex/Alamy; **p82** (b) © Warren Photographic; 86 (t) © Dave Bevan/Alamy; **p88** (b) © Tom Tookey/Alamy; **p90** (b) © Warren Photographic; **p92-93** © Geoff Wilkinson/Alamy

Additional designs by Karen Tomlins and Laura Hammonds
Cover design by Joanne Kirkby
Digital manipulation by Keith Furnival

Additional illustrations by John Barber, Lizzie Barber, Reuben Barrance, Joyce Bee, Trevor Boyer, Hilary Burn, Kuo Kang Chen, Aziz Khan, Tim Hayward, Alan Male, Andy Martin, Annabel Milne, David Palmer, Julie Piper, Chris Shields, Peter Stebbing, Phil Weire and others

This edition first published in 2014 by Usborne Publishing Ltd, 83-85 Saffron Hill, London EC1N 8RT. www.usborne.com Copyright © 2014, 2008 Usborne Publishing Ltd. The name Usborne and the devices ♀⚲ are Trade Marks of Usborne Publishing Ltd. All rights reserved. No part of this publication may be reproduced, stored in a retrieval system or transmitted in any form or by any means, electronic, mechanical, photocopying, recording or otherwise, without the prior permission of the publisher. UKE. Printed in China.